Law of Attraction for Motivation

How to Get and Stay Motivated to Attract the Life You Have Always Wanted and Be Unstoppable

By Elena G.Rivers

Copyright Elena G.Rivers © 2019

All rights reserved. No part of this publication may be reproduced, stored in a retrieval system, or transmitted, in any form or by any means, electronic, mechanical, photocopying, recording or otherwise, without the prior written permission of the author and the publishers.

The scanning, uploading, and distribution of this book via the Internet, or via any other means, without the permission of the author is illegal and punishable by law. Please purchase only authorized electronic editions, and do not participate in or encourage electronic piracy of copyrighted materials.

All information in this book has been carefully researched and checked for factual accuracy. However, the author and publishers make no warranty, expressed or implied, that the information contained herein is appropriate for every individual, situation or purpose, and assume no responsibility for errors or omission. The reader assumes the risk and full responsibility for all actions, and the author will not be held liable for any loss or damage, whether consequential, incidental, and special or otherwise, that may result from the information presented in this publication.

Disclaimer Notice:

Please note the information contained in this document is for educational and entertainment purposes only. Every attempt has been made to provide accurate, up to date and completely reliable information. No warranties of any kind are expressed or implied.ized.

Readers acknowledge that the author is not engaging in the rendering of legal, financial, medical or professional advice. By reading this document, the reader agrees that under no circumstances are we responsible for any losses, direct or indirect, which are incurred as a result of the use of information contained within this document, including, but not limited to, errors, omissions, or inaccuracies.

Contents

Introduction 7
A Special Offer from Elena to Help You Manifest Faster 22
Chapter 1 24
Reconnecting with Your Inner Guidance 24
Chapter 2 37
Vision for Life and Vision Boards 37
The Mistakes to Avoid 37
Chapter 3 54
The # 1 Motivation Killer and How to Mindfully Release It to Live Your Best Life 54
    Intrinsic vs Extrinsic Motivation 60
    The Self-Love for Motivation 65
    Trust the Process and Love Every Minute of it. 72
Chapter 4 74
The Mental and Emotional Peeling to Welcome the New and Get Rid of the Old 74
    Releasing Pressure and Judgment to Feel Free and Naturally Motivated 79
Chapter 5 82

How to Deal with Adversity and Keep Taking
Inspired Action 82
　How to Deal with Self-Sabotage 89
Chapter 7 93
The Best LOA Tools to Stay Motivated 93
　Mindful Exercises to Raise Your Vibration First
　Thing in the Morning 95
　The Power of Mindful Journaling 95
　Meditation to Stay Motivated? 100
Conclusion 105
A Special Offer from Elena 107
More Books written by Elena G.Rivers 109

Introduction

Thank you for taking an interest in this book. It really means a lot to me. My name is Elena and I am a Law of Attraction nerd and author with a passion for holistic self-help.

Even though right now I am blessed with a life I love, as well the opportunity to share my passion and knowledge with others, it wasn't always like that.

My life used to be a mess and it was a vicious cycle of pain, rejection and addictions. I was desperate for answers for myself because I wanted to create a better life for myself and those around me.

That got me on a path of never-ending study. I started devouring self-help and spiritual resources and working with all kinds of mentors, from business and success coaches to energy healers.

I became committed to transforming my life. As I was going deeper and deeper into the materials and seminars I was learning from, I quickly realized that some resources were very superficial and mainstream and were not helping me at all. After reading a ton of books about success, motivation, productivity and similar topics, I knew that I even though I had learned a ton of new concepts, something was missing. Something was missing because

LAW OF ATTRACTION FOR MOTIVATION

I got to a point where I felt stuck and confused. It felt like I could never make a long-lasting change. I would witness other people's success and transformation and it seemed like they were motivated and unstoppable, but I felt like a dumb turtle (no offense to turtles, I think they are very cute).

To sum up, I felt like the mainstream world of high performance, business mindset, and strictly financial success self-development world was not providing me with the answers I was searching for.

My main question was, *How does one become truly unstoppable?* What is this invisible force that can keep you going but at the same time, when not used properly, can wear you down? And finally, I wanted to know how to unleash my full potential, but from a place of self-approval and authenticity. I got sick and tired of pursuing careers just to make those around me think I was something special while I was feeling empty and drained inside.

I knew I was going to face my dark side and many issues that I needed to work through. Luckily, I also knew it would be a change for the better and that it would be a lasting one.

And so, I began exploring the world of the Law of Attraction, Spirituality, Energy, Reiki and the Subconscious Mind.

LAW OF ATTRACTION FOR MOTIVATION

Eventually I came to a simple conclusion: self-development in itself will not work unless you work on your energy and shift it to a place of authenticity, self-love and following your inner voice.

And this is exactly what I teach through all my books. My mission is to explain the self-development concepts of personal success, focus, happiness, wellness, productivity and motivation, using the Law of Attraction and the re-alignment of yourself with your true core.

Please note that this doesn't mean we will be just visualizing and reciting some affirmations. It means that we will go much, much deeper, so that you can get rid of layers that may be preventing you from becoming the best version of yourself and living your purpose.

To unleash your true motivations, the first thing that needs to take place is healing. Healing of past traumas, mistakes and fears you may be facing. Healing is a normal process that consists of peaks and valleys. To be fully healed, you need to give yourself permission to face some truths that may feel uncomfortable at first. I am here to help you with that in a non-judgmental way.

Creating long-lasting motivation is not like taking a pill. It's a process. The good news is that this process has the power to truly transform your life, career and relationships. It can help you get back to your true self. You will be able to step into your courage and no longer fear other people's opinions and judgements.

As we go through the process I share in this book, I want you to imagine that I am gently holding your hand through each and every step. Even if today you're having a bad day, don't worry, you are totally allowed to. Just relax, enjoy the process and let it be without forcing anything.

The best things manifest themselves when you are not pushing, forcing and hustling. The best reality emerges when you are *allowing* while taking meaningful and purposeful action in alignment with your true motivation. This is what this book will help you discover. Your deep motivation.

How This Book Came About

After undergoing my own radical transformation in all areas of my life- health, career, finance and relationships, using deep LOA concepts, I made it my purpose to share and teach, using my books to share my message.

The idea for this book, which is a motivation/ Law of Attraction combo, was born after I noticed a pattern that prevents many people from living their best, authentic and happy life. And that pattern is "I lost my motivation, I lost my driving force, I don't feel like doing anything."

What very often happens is that people try to remedy this issue by trying harder. Or they turn to "gurus" who begin shaming them or calling them lazy. However, the root of the problem is very simple and it's not even a problem to be honest…it's a question of perception and knowing the correct order of things to focus on.

You see, most people pursue goals that are not even their own goals. They very often set goals in order to feel worthy in front of other people or to make other people happy. And since the goal is not really connected to their true vision, it feels like they always have to push and hustle to make something out of themselves. After some time, that "rat race" can turn into a burnout, both physical as well as emotional.

I am going to give you a sense of freedom now by telling you that it's okay to lose your motivation and you should not be ashamed of doing so. It's simply a sign that your subconscious mind is sending you. And that sign means that the goal you are pursuing may not be for you. It may also mean that the goal you are going after is for you, but you are sending out way too much importance and therefore creating a sense of resistance that pushes your results away, making you lose motivation in the process.

LAW OF ATTRACTION FOR MOTIVATION

For example, a person on a date with someone they really, really like. They try so hard that the person they are on a date with feels lots of pressure and is not interested in another date.

Or, imagine a person with a pet, for example, a cat. If they start to stroke it too much, the cat will push them away.

Or, a person goes on a job interview and tries so hard that they come off as being too full of themselves, or too nervous.

Another sense of freedom I am going to give you now, in this introduction (it's still not the main meal), is that nobody is perfect.

There are many self-help gurus out there, gurus of all kinds, from business to spirituality. They all have a meticulously curated image on social media, they are always perfect, they are always doing the right thing and they never have a bad day.

You look them up online and you automatically start comparing yourself to what you see. This results in two possible scenarios:

1. You lose your motivation, thinking, "I will never be like them, so what's the point?"
2. You do the opposite, you take "massive action" and you try too hard while burning yourself out.

LAW OF ATTRACTION FOR MOTIVATION

A friend of mine who wanted to be a famous influencer on social media, and grow all his social media platforms at the same time, burned himself out. He was comparing himself with big, famous gurus who have teams of people who help them create and post content, optimize their platforms and grow their following.

The problem? He was attempting to do that all by himself, while still working in a full-time job. Eventually he burned out and it took him a few months to recover. After going through the process I will be sharing in this book, he decided that to achieve big things, he had to start small and that he had to stop comparing himself to other people.

Finally, he realized that he didn't really care that much about fame or the number of followers he had. His personal goal was to have a job quitting income so that he could go full time with his passion while creating content and promoting products that help people.

He also realized he didn't need to have a big following but rather a following of people who really resonated with his message.

In alignment with that discovery, he simply focused on one social media platform and stopped comparing himself with big name gurus who very often spend 50 k a month on professional teams and paid advertisement to grow their social media platforms.

LAW OF ATTRACTION FOR MOTIVATION

Does that mean he is not ambitious or is shooting too low? No. It means that he's going through a step-by-step process to grow a following at his own pace.

Another example: A person who is just getting started on a health and fitness journey may have a simple goal of losing some weight and cleaning up their diet. If they start comparing themselves with big name professional athletes, who, once again, have teams of doctors, nutritionists and high-performance coaches around them to monitor and measure what they do, eat etc. well...it will be very hard to compete with that, right?

A person who is simply looking for a side income, or wants to replace their job income with a small business that is more aligned with their passion, should not compare themselves with someone who is a multi-millionaire. Well, yes, they can use someone's success story as inspiration as for what is possible, and they can hold that vision. But...everything is a process that takes time. By trying to go too fast, you may end up burning yourself out and losing your motivation or even thinking you are not good enough.

Today, many of us want instant gratification and we overlook the importance of simple, step by step dedication.

It's time to change your relationship with the concept of motivation and accept a few truths:

LAW OF ATTRACTION FOR MOTIVATION

1. Emotions that we may perceive as negative, such as not feeling motivated, are simply signs to help you get on the right track and re-align your actions, energy and thoughts using the Law of Attraction. (This is what the following chapters of this book teach.)
2. These emotions may also be telling you that you need to slow down.
3. You need to give yourself permission to stop thinking about what other people may think of you. That will allow you to set up goals that really excite you.
4. Real, holistic motivation is like a muscle that can be worked on. It's like going to the gym- you need to have a plan that is easy to follow, however that plan can't be about overworking and exhausting yourself. It must be sustainable. If you are new to it, you can't compare yourself to all those "gym rats" out there, whether it's a real gym, or an emotional / motivational gym.
5. You must be patient and believe in the process, but at the same time be impatient with the small, everyday actions you can take.

This is exactly what we will be discussing in this book while combing it with very practical Law of Attraction exercises.

Most readers who turn to my books have already been through a ton of entrepreneur as well as self-help materials and they have tried everything under the sun. And most of them, after going through my humble materials, discover that the goals and ventures they wanted to manifest were not even what they truly wanted.

They either wanted to impress someone or get some title or achievement to post on social media to feel worthy. I know, I know. Sounds a bit cruel. I was in that mindset for years, even before social media came along. I worked very hard, even when I was totally burned out, just because I wanted to achieve goals that were totally out of alignment with what I truly wanted to impress people who didn't even care about me.

All the meaningless and superficial achievement I was chasing was just to feel worthy and accepted by other people. I created my own mental prison and it took me years to get rid of it.

(My full story and the process I used to get back to alignment with self-love is something I talk about in depth in my book: Self-Love Handbook magnified with the Law of Attraction. I highly recommend that you read it if you're seeking deeper healing and connection with yourself to get back in alignment.)

Some readers are looking for motivation to transform their health and fitness. They have already tried all the diets out there only to end up confused and burned out. However, after going through the process I teach in this book, and by combining holistic motivation with the Law of Attraction, they could finally dive deep, listen to their body and create a healthy lifestyle they enjoy.

Some readers were able to use the process taught in this book to finally get involved in a creative or artistic activity they always wanted to pursue, like for example writing, music or art. By getting connected to your true desires and motivations, you also diminish the fear of rejection and criticism. You allow yourself to keep going even on a bad day. In fact, those bad days are just signs from the Universe to put us to a test and see if we are really passionate about what we do.

And don't worry if this doesn't make any sense now. After going through this book, you will know exactly what to do and how to do it to be unstoppable in your own unique way. (Some people around you will be under the impression that you've got some magical powers, trust me on that one- but the best part is that they will feel inspired by your actions.)

Let's be honest – motivation comes easily when things are going our way, we are getting results we have worked for and we are riding the wave of success. Then we feel like celebrating and taking more action to achieve even better results.

We feel excited about what we do, and motivation comes naturally.

LAW OF ATTRACTION FOR MOTIVATION

The problem is, how do we stay motivated and consistent when things are a bit slow? How do we maintain the right mindset and keep going when life hasn't treated us well? What should we do when things get tough, the only thing we manifest is failure and we begin losing our passion?

Obstacles very often cause us to lose our motivation, and unfortunately, while there are many gurus who have speeches, seminars, books and other resources to help *you get motivated*, very few of those resources talk about *how to maintain* that motivation and what to do when things don't pick up as fast as we originally envisioned they would.

This is where I come in, to help you through this book. This is not yet another motivational book that you will read, feel good about for a few days but never feel inspired to take action or to create lasting transformation. This book is designed as a step-by-step transformational action guide to help you grow your motivational muscle using a holistic mix of the Law of Attraction, quantum physics, mindfulness, balanced self-care to stay nourished and energized as well as re-connecting with your subconscious mind on a deeper level. Most importantly it's about getting rid of the superficial layers and other people's negative energies and expectations that are holding you back.

LAW OF ATTRACTION FOR MOTIVATION

The exercises taught in this book will also help you improve your personal productivity and focus. As a result, you will feel inspired to walk away from people, circumstances, events and even social media channels that might be draining your motivation.

Motivation can be compared to eating a healthy diet and living a healthy lifestyle. You need to commit to the whole package on a regular basis. It's hard to lose weight by only eating healthily occasionally, or by not doing any physical activity. At the same time, it's very hard to transform your health if you eat some healthy food here and there but never decide to eliminate foods that are making you sick and tired.

One thing to remember though- it's not about being perfect. You can live a healthy lifestyle and eat a healthy, clean food diet, yet every now and then indulge in pizza or a cake. Same with motivation. Once again, let me stress- some days will be less motivating and less "on track". Motivation is like a muscle, and it also needs some rest days. The problem is when there are too many of those rest days in a row and we start feeling guilty or feel like quitting what we were doing.

Most motivational books don't work because they offer information on a very superficial level. They never make you dive deep to help you realize what actually depletes you of energy and motivation so that you can get to the root of the problem and get rid of whatever is holding you back.

Taking action if very important, but most self-help books forget about taking an inspired, aligned and meaningful action. Action that helps you stay energized instead of burning you out. So, after consuming some more mainstream motivational content, you may start feeling bad about yourself thinking, "What's wrong with me? Why am I going so slowly? This guru really seems to be always getting it right. Why can't I be like them?"

Deep inside you may be even rebelling against another motivational quote or another "Just take massive action and hustle all day" cliché.

Well, the good news is this: if you can make a conscious decision that you really want to change your relationship with motivation and dive deep through this Law of Attraction for Motivation journey, this book will help you for years to come.

My biggest intention is to help you redesign your vision and goals (this is where LOA will be very handy) so that the motivation you create will not be short lived. It will be automatic, almost subconscious, as you start working through the different emotional layers that are holding you back from achieving your goals.

LAW OF ATTRACTION FOR MOTIVATION

As humans, we have every capacity to live proactive, deliberate, self-actualized and fun lives. We can show our failures who is in charge, bag up our fears and turn them into this invisible force that keeps us going. We can become the screenwriters of our own lives and redesign what we don't like – or want to change.

But most importantly, you will change your perception and see everything that happened *to you* as something that happened *for you*. In other words, you will master the art of turning all kinds of circumstances into motivational fuel to help you be unstoppable.

Are you ready to take it a step further and ROCK ON in *your* life, career, fitness goals, and whatever other endeavors in your near (and far) future? I want you to achieve your goals, not someone else's goals, so that you can achieve true happiness and fulfilment in your life.

A Special Offer from Elena to Help You Manifest Faster

Before we get into Motivation, I would like to offer you a free access to my VIP newsletter:

Visit the link below to learn more:

www.loaforsuccess.com/home

******

OR CLICK HERE

When you sign up, you will instantly receive a free copy of an exclusive LOA Workbook that will help you raise your vibration in 5 days or less:

You will also be the first one to learn about my new releases, bonuses and other valuable resources to help you on your journey.

Sign up now and I'll "see you" in the first email. I am looking forward to connecting with you.

Love,

Elena

Chapter 1

Reconnecting with Your Inner Guidance

The first step in the process is reconnecting with your inner guidance. And the best way to do so is to allow yourself to design your ideal day and reconnect yourself with that vision on a regular basis, so that your inner GPS can guide you, while keeping your motivation levels high.

Please do this exercise without any attachment or expectations. Do it as a simple experiment.

The word *experiment* implies that there is no right or wrong. You cannot fail with an experiment, because all you get from it is data, right?

This is exactly what we want to do now.

It's time to dive deep and create your ideal day, while getting rid of all the layers, negative associations and all those annoying voices in your head as "but how can I do it?"

LAW OF ATTRACTION FOR MOTIVATION

The exercises I will share with you can always be slightly changed over time. What I like to do is to give you different options so that you can pick and choose and focus on something that works best for you.

Tracking back my successes and failures, I can honestly tell you that, whenever I was successful, I would in some way do this kind of an exercise. Even before I knew about it and even before I got into the Law of Attraction, my mind was doing a very similar kind of an exercise. Then, of course, I felt very motivated and inspired to take action that was aligned with my vision.

At the same time, whenever I would experience long periods of feeling stuck, anxious or even depressed (yea, I am a positive person by nature, but I also have my ups and downs), it was because I lacked clarity and confidence in my action. Needless to say, that was draining my energy, productivity and motivation.

I would just take random actions without focus, self-awareness and vision. And again, it was when I was skipping the exercise I am just about to share with you. I would either get stuck in my mind thinking that it was no longer necessary or thinking that it was only for beginners or other similar excuses.

LAW OF ATTRACTION FOR MOTIVATION

You may be thinking, but Elena, just show me how I can be motivated right here and right now and then I can go out there and change everything in my life.

But it usually goes the other way around and big changes start in your mind. Same with fitness, nobody can teach you how to be fit right here and right now. They can give you steps for you to work on your muscles, diet and also your mindset so that you have a blueprint you can use to transform yourself on a deeper level.

Motivation and self-image are like siblings. No big changes can be made without working on your subconscious mind. Your subconscious mind is a mechanism designed to keep you in what it thinks is your comfort zone. It has good intentions and it wants to protect you.

We are where we are because of our self-image. And as harsh as it may sound, our results equal our self-image and our motivation is a by-product of that.

Everyone creates something and some kind of a life and results. But whether it's the results they actually really wanted or not, is a different story. Most people just run on an autopilot, moving between careers they hate and self-imposed distractions to entertain themselves in between. Of course, some people are happy where they are. But you are here because you are into conscious living and you are looking for big changes and transformations in all areas of your life while creating a positive impact.

It's important to design your ideal day in your mind and write down all the details. Believe it or not, I used to be very sceptical about it. I would laugh at all of that rejecting it as some "woo-woo" and would even say, "Just show me how to stay motivated, be successful and make money and then I will be able to do whatever I want. Just give me the shortcut, give me the pill."

And so, I worked hard and hard and harder and harder and it all worked well for a while. But eventually I reached mental and emotional confusion. I got stuck on the same level. As a desperate way out, I began to compulsively look for strategies, and gurus. Of course, skills are important, but here's the thing…I lost clarity.

At some point I disconnected from myself and forgot about my why and my vision. All days were busy and disconnected. Friendships were rare and very superficial. Then, I realized that I had created a reality that was a prison, not freedom, because I was viewing money and success as end goals, not as tools.

So, I got back to doing the lifestyle design exercise to reconnect with my true motivation.

LAW OF ATTRACTION FOR MOTIVATION

I know, I know. You may be thinking, "Oh, but Elena, I don't have clarity...not too sure what my ideal day looks like."

Well, don't worry. Even if you feel uncertain now, as long as you set up a small goal, a micro habit if you will, to sit down every day, and journal for even five minutes and just write down the details of your ideal day and try to feel them, live them and focus on the positive emotions you experience, you will be able to unblock and unstick yourself. It's not that you have to sit down and logically come up with the best version of your ideal day. Just start now, do it, and as you get more ideas, feel free to add them. It's really lots of fun.

Do you know what the most successful athletes do to stay motivated? Before the game or the event, they visualize the process and the successful outcome, they focus on their feelings and live it in their mind. They also do it after the game! Yes, whether the result was positive or negative, in their mind, they replay it as positive (if the game went well) to further anchor those feelings. If they game was not successful, they create their own replay where the result is successful. It's a technique based on the Law of Attraction, a technique that is free and effective.

So, no matter what happens, in their mind, at least two out of three games are successful. And if the real game is successful, they make it a triple success.

LAW OF ATTRACTION FOR MOTIVATION

Coaches who specialize in high performance and training athletes, know the tricks of the subconscious mind. It's the invisible force that connects to our self-image and leads us towards some positive results.

Take a piece of paper and a pen, and if you are new to journaling, set up a timer to make sure you fully focus on this task and get in a flow. Make sure you avoid distractions and switch off your phone etc. I suggest you don't use your computer. Just a pen and paper.

Now, take a few deep breaths and allow yourself to think big. Some people struggle to be able to create a step-by-step process for their ideal day. Like, it's hard for them to come up with events on a timeline. That's fine. I am also the same way. You can always journal random events from your ideal day.

Maybe the first thing that comes to your mind is a nice lunch out with your partner, enjoying the sunshine somewhere sunny and warm, ordering the food you love without checking the price tag.

Perhaps you want to go full time with your passion. Well, imagine yourself doing that for a living. Maybe you want to create an image of you, your camera and your amazing YouTube audience. You read comments you get from your tribe and feel happy. As you create that feeling, something else may come up in your mind.

LAW OF ATTRACTION FOR MOTIVATION

Think of it as a slide that you create. You can always arrange the slides in the order that you want.

For example, you imagine that someone calls you, offering you a speaking gig or wanting to hire you as a coach. You attract new business opportunities and meet new business partners.

From that slide, another slide may come to your mind…you wake up in a hotel, new location. You hear seagulls. You love traveling and speaking, getting paid to talk about what you are passionate about.

One of my slides is writing while overlooking the sea. Receiving emails from happy readers and being happy because of their transformations. Making a difference through my books and helping other people overcome obstacles and avoid my early mistakes. I can smell the ocean; the sound of the waves is calming.

Now, I live a one-hour drive from the ocean, so whenever I go to the beach, I try to merge myself with my vision while expressing my gratitude.

There's something else I do because I know that the subconscious mind loves this kind of "games". When writing at home, I listen to YouTube videos that contain the sound of the waves and the ocean.

LAW OF ATTRACTION FOR MOTIVATION

Also, whenever I travel, I try to upgrade my room to a place where I can enjoy the sound of the waves and the beach. I imagine it's my own house.

You will have details coming up. Some may seem unrealistic, but don't think about *how*, just focus on the *why*. Feel worthy and deserving right here, right now.

Write everything down.

When do you wake up?

What does your bedroom look like?

Where do you live? City? Nature? Penthouse, villa, a cosy apartment?

Who do you live with?

Children? Spouse? Pets?

What is your morning routine? What do you love doing?

Maybe you have a personal trainer and nutritionist?

Do you wake up in a clean, organized space?

LAW OF ATTRACTION FOR MOTIVATION

Do you hire someone who cleans your house? What about your office? Where do you work?

When and where do you eat your lunch?

What do you do in the afternoon?

What passions can you pursue?

What does it feel like?

When you do this exercise every day, even if you do it a disorganized, random "slide" way, you will eventually create an image and a movie that will fall into a step-by-step daily routine of your dream day.

What I also love about this exercise is that you can see the future you that is a stronger version of the current you. The new you has better habits and a better mindset. What you can start doing is to adopt your future habits right now. This is how you will bridge the new you with the current you and launch the new version of yourself. Eventually, what you see as your dream vision now will become your reality. Your subconscious mind will get comfortable with it and will push you like an invisible force to take action.

LAW OF ATTRACTION FOR MOTIVATION

A friend of mine, who is an expert in sales and marketing, uses a similar exercise on a regular basis. Many people turn to him because they don't feel successful in sales, and they hope to learn some new techniques to help them get over it. But in most cases, it's not the new technique that needs work, but their motivation, confidence, self-image and mindset.

Here's a great exercise I learned from him, and you can add it to your motivation toolkit whenever dealing with a new stressful situation that requires you to leave your comfort zone. It can be a sales call, pitching someone or even getting interviewed.

Imagine exactly what you are wearing on the occasion you are preparing yourself for. Perhaps the occasion is a sales call, interview, athletic performance or talking to a stranger.

Are you wearing any jewellery? How do you feel? How do you feel while talking? Do not overcomplicate it in terms of what you will say, exactly word for word. That will make you nervous. It will feel like reciting something. Instead, focus on the feelings that may come to your mind as you are being interviewed, working out or talking to a stranger (depending on what situation you are imagining).

Keep that feeling inside you, by replaying the parts you especially enjoyed in your mind. Whenever you feel down, close your eyes and focus on people who make you feel good and appreciate you. In business, it can be people like your regular clients, or business partners you admire.

If your goal is to create a healthy, fit body, then imagine walking down the street and wearing your favourite clothes while getting compliments from other people who feel inspired by your transformation and also want to transform.

Create a slide of that feeling and re-use it whenever you feel like it. Whenever you feel down. Most people focus on the negative and on what they don't want. Ever since I started to focus on that simple trick while at the same time writing, "I attract amazing people to my private and professional life" in my journal, I gave myself permission to leave negative environments and made new friendships, on and offline, friendships that aligned better with the new, improved edition of myself that I wanted to launch.

Your action plan to get and stay motivated
It's very important that you do the exercises from this chapter every day, even if it's just for a few minutes every day. Most subconscious mind experts recommend doing them after waking up or before you go to bed, or both. You can accompany this with reading your goals (goals you really want, not someone else's goals and expectations).

LAW OF ATTRACTION FOR MOTIVATION

Remember- we have feelings and emotions. We can be programmed like computers, and feelings and emotions do give us an advantage. By working with your feelings and emotions the right way, you get to improve your self-image by making your subconscious mind comfortable with the uncomfortable and the unknown. Once your subconscious mind starts to feel confident, you will feel confident and you'll perform confident actions.

It's very likely you will encounter negative voices in your head like "I can't do it" or, "I will never be able to..." Remember it's just a test. You can easily turn those questions around by asking, yourself:

-How can I do it?
-Who can help me?
-What is my next step?

Keep re-aligning yourself with your vision, by feeling and /or visualizing the random "slides" from your ideal day.

It can be:
"I am walking my dog on the beach and then we go back to my big beach house."
"I am on a plane traveling to a conference where I am a speaker. I feel so excited."

LAW OF ATTRACTION FOR MOTIVATION

"I am in the gym, after a great workout, feeling so amazing. Other people ask me for tips and motivation. It feels so good that my efforts are finally manifesting as the healthy fit body I always wanted."

You can write these down, read them aloud, or even record yourself on your phone and listen to yourself. You can also close your eyes and visualize or meditate on the feeling you are experiencing, while giving yourself the gift of shifting yourself to your ideal day.

You are now connecting yourself to your Invisible Motivational Force that will keep you going in your courageous attempts to manifest your dream life.

The next step will take it to the next level by combining the random pieces of your ideal day into a holistic vision board to help you stay motivated while transforming all areas of your life.

Chapter 2

Vision for Life and Vision Boards

The Mistakes to Avoid

If you have ever consumed any success, self-help, business, high performance of even classical LOA materials, you probably already know that in order to be successful with your goals, you need to know what you want.

It's not hard to make a vision board.

It's not hard to write down what you think you want.

And it's not hard to record what you want and turn your desires into affirmations and meditations.

All the above-mentioned techniques are amazing if you actually know what you want, and it comes from you, from your core.

The problem? Most people don't know what they really want, even if they intellectually think they do. Very often people get into spirituality and LOA because they are looking for something else out there. Maybe they got burned out in their corporate jobs or careers.

LAW OF ATTRACTION FOR MOTIVATION

Or maybe they spent years trying to achieve their goals and when they did, they ended up feeling miserable and unhappy.

So how do you become clear on what you want? How will you know whether what you want comes from yourself? First of all, you need to be very careful about what you put into your mind.

The #1 mistake that most people make with LOA is that instead of diving deeply into this step, they create their vision board really fast, without even checking if that vision truly comes from their hearts. Then, they try hard to manifest. Another mistake. Trying too hard sends the following signal to the Universe: "I don't have it, it's not for me, I need to work harder because I don't have it."

My number one recommendation when it comes to creating your vision is this: Take some time off. Allow yourself to be your only friend for a few days. Go to a town you have never been to. You need some time and space to think about what you really want. If you can't take a few days off, just allow yourself a few long walks after or before work. Go somewhere peaceful and quiet. Allow yourself to think. Write down all your goals for every area of life:

Health & Fitness
Energy & Vitality
Spirituality and Contribution
Work & Career

LAW OF ATTRACTION FOR MOTIVATION

Finance & Money
Relationships & Love
Friendships
Passion & Hobby
Travel, Party and Fun

Go through all the above-mentioned areas of life, and start writing down everything that comes to your mind. Then, come back to that vision later. Read through it and question everything you put on paper. Do it in a mindful way, without judging yourself. Keep asking yourself:

"Is it good for me, will it make me happy? Is that what I really want?"

Finally, ask yourself, "Are all areas of my life in harmony?"
For example, a social life that involves lots of partying and drinking may interfere with your health and fitness goals. This will confuse you and the Universe. Needless to say, you will start losing your motivation and feeling like you're not making any progress.

One of my early mistakes with LOA was that out of fear, I created a dozen different vision boards that did not really connect to the same vision. Different vision boards with different houses and lifestyles.

LAW OF ATTRACTION FOR MOTIVATION

I was thinking that any of them would be good for me. I guessed that by doing a shotgun approach I would at least be able to manifest something. Eventually something will materialize, right?

Wrong, wrong, wrong! A shotgun approach to manifesting will only make you burn out. A sniper approach works so much better! More on that later in this book.

Not surprisingly, during that time, I tried different business ventures. All of them failed. I invested a ton of money and never made any money. I could never commit to one idea.

Now, when it comes to creating your LOA abundance vision and manifesting the motivation level you want, the focus you need to adopt is the same kind of focus that the best high performers as well as spiritual leaders apply. It's better to have fewer goals but strong ones. You want goals that are really yours.

Take a few deep notes from your heart.

YOU, your motivation. Your feelings and your emotions.

You see, what you want is really a reflection of your feelings and emotions. Most people don't focus on their core but instead they just jump straight into creating a vision board. Using what I like to call a "rat race strategy".

LAW OF ATTRACTION FOR MOTIVATION

Ok, lemmee see. The Joneses got a new car, so let me go on Pinterest and find something and put it on my vision board and manifest it.

There is nothing wrong with wanting to have a nice car, I also like nice things. The question is- do you really care about that car? Or do you want it because someone you look up to cares about it?

Maybe what you are really looking for is a sense of freedom and wealth? Knowing that you have enough to get a nice "toy" when you please? But at the same not being too attached to it?

A former client of mine had a vision board with a beach house on it. I asked her, "Why did you put it there? How do you feel about it?"
She said, "Well, I guess my parents would like it."
I asked, "What makes you think so?"
She said, "Because it's a house of someone who is successful and has a secure career. My parents would be proud of me if I had such a house."

Can you see where it's going? No wonder she struggled with motivation. The big beach house wasn't really her goal. She just wanted a peaceful life with a creative career she's passionate about and a cozy city apartment.

LAW OF ATTRACTION FOR MOTIVATION

After a deep talk we realized that she didn't even care about a fancy beach house. Nor did she care about a job in sales. What she really cared about was establishing a stronger bond with her family and feeling accepted for who she is.

Keep asking yourself:
-Why?
-Why do I want it?
-How does it make me feel?

The second round of questions is:
-Does it make me feel light?
-Does it make me feel heavy?

In most cases, when you start off feeling heavy that vision is not your vision but someone else's. Other people may be quick at manifesting it, and maybe you thought you "could try too". Yes, you could, but is it right for you?

These are my recommendations for you to go through before you start creating your vision board:

-Allow yourself some time off and get connected to your true feelings and emotions. Meditate, walk in nature, take Epsom salt baths.

LAW OF ATTRACTION FOR MOTIVATION

-Start off by asking yourself what would make you happy. Materialistic goals are fine if they are coming from you because you feel joy while being surrounded by the objects you want to manifest.

However, if the root of your goal comes from insecurity and not feeling worthy or trying to impress the Jones's then I recommend you redefine your vision. Otherwise you will quickly lose your motivation and may end up feeling burned out.

-After you have built those fundamentals in your imagination, set the intention to create a very simple and basic vision board, with just a few simple images that will not confuse your conscious and subconscious mind.

-Does it make you feel lighter or heavier? Of course, lighter should be the answer.

-As you go through this process, be sure to take care of your emotional state. Have an Epsom salt bath or get a massage if you have been having a stressful day. It's hard to align yourself with your vision if you're feeling stressed out and there is no point in creating a vision board just for the sake of doing it.

LAW OF ATTRACTION FOR MOTIVATION

Okay, ready? Now that we have done the hard part, it's time for the fun part- making the vision board that is truly yours.

The images for your vision board can be cut out from magazines, or printed from online platforms. The only important thing to keep in mind is that the images must speak to you. Make sure they evoke a powerful feeling of joy, satisfaction and even a little fear (which is fine, because our best dreams can be scary!). That vision board will be with you for years, and the best part is that the You from the future is already looking at it with a sense of accomplishment thinking, "Wow, I can't believe it all is true now." Stay in that feeling for as long as possible. Take a few deep breaths, be mindful and enjoy this step.

According to the Law of Attraction, in this moment, all the possibilities exist and what you want is already here. It's just a question of aligning yourself to your vision with your thoughts, feelings and actions.

Put several images of your perfect vision on a piece of poster board. Put this vision board in your plain view, in a place where you can see it regularly. I even framed my vision board and placed it next to my main bathroom mirror.

LAW OF ATTRACTION FOR MOTIVATION

Wherever you place your vision board. Look at it often, revel in it, and ask yourself, "How am I going to make these visions come true?"

Once you have your vision board, look at each individual picture. Start with picture number one. Ask yourself, "What can I do today, this week and this month to get closer to my vision? What is the new, more empowered version of myself doing?"

Let's say it is a picture of your dream home.

Ask yourself why you need to have a home like that and when do you need to have it? Who will you share it with? What does it feel and smell like? What do you do for a living? How much time do you spend in your new home? Do you have any pets? Do you clean it yourself or do you hire help?

Keep asking yourself, "What does it feel like?"

That will help you stay excited about pursuing a new job or career that can help you manifest the amount of money you need to start living in your dream house.

Perhaps you think about some family planning and talk to your wife or husband about expanding your family to complete your vision.

LAW OF ATTRACTION FOR MOTIVATION

Now, have a look at another picture. Maybe it's a picture of a healthy lifestyle, like a person who is really fit and working out. Ask yourself, "What does it feel like? What daily habits does this person have? What can I do today to get closer to my vision?"

Making your vision board opens up a world of possibilities to you and your dreams. It truly is a blank canvas to paint your own reality. You may even find dreams that you didn't know you have. I did! For example, a few years ago, I didn't know I would be a writer. As a teenager, someone who was an authority figure for me criticized my writing. Because of that I abstained from writing for nearly three decades. It was only after going through my own radical transformation with the Law of Attraction that I realized I wanted to become a writer.

On my vision board, I put a few words like:

Freedom

Creativity

Contribution

Self-Expression

Peace of Mind

LAW OF ATTRACTION FOR MOTIVATION

After "meditating" with my vision board for a few months and constantly asking myself deep questions, I concluded that I could combine Freedom, Creativity, Contribution and Self-Expression as well as Peace of Mind by becoming a writer.

And you know what was incredibly crazy and amazing? I *loved* it. Suddenly, everyone cheered me on. When I started, I was feeling emotionally shaky from my previous fear of being rejected and laughed at.

The point of this story is this: sometimes you may not even know what your dreams and motivations are. That is why it's so important to allow yourself to find them, using mindful Law of Attraction exercises and creating your vision board and going through it every day. Vision boarding helps you envision what truly makes you happy and fulfilled and lets you play with it. It's like a puzzle game.

You can make your goals happen in the truest and best version you can. All the dreams are there, waiting for you. You just have to narrow down life's many options and decide what it is that you want to go after.

Aside from attraction, there is also action. Especially mindful, purposeful and inspired action. After all, you don't want to burn yourself out.

LAW OF ATTRACTION FOR MOTIVATION

It's time to make a simple plan you enjoy. You want to focus on simple actions you get to repeat on a regular basis. Let's say that your goal is to create a healthy, fit body.

Your three big monthly goals could be:
-Sign up for the gym.
-Organize your schedule in such a way that you can work out three times a week.
-Research healthy meal prep and decide whether you will cook your meals or whether it makes sense for you to hire someone who can help you.

Your three big weekly goals could be:
- Work out on Monday, Wednesday and Friday.
- Pick up healthy meals and green juice on Tuesday and Thursday.
- Be in bed early and listen to guided meditations to fall asleep.

Daily goals:
1. Go to the gym.
2. Make a healthy green smoothie for today and tomorrow.
3. Stretch before going to sleep and practice gratitude.

LAW OF ATTRACTION FOR MOTIVATION

No matter what, get specific with the details of what you need to happen. The Universe is fond of specifics– and once you put these details and desires out into the Universe and set a plan to go after these visions, watch the details and opportunities start to flow your way.

The final step to your vision board process is to, well, en*vision* what your dreams (and life) will be like once you have achieved them. In other words, what will your life look like once you have your ideal home or your super-healthy, fit body?

How will you walk and dress? Who will you hang out with? Use your senses to really, really imagine what your life will be like with your dreams come true. Smell the ocean, picture the look on your spouse's face when you tell them about the new goal you have achieved. Envision your own confidence level, as you will have created something incredible in your life such as achieving your fitness goals and inspiring those around you. You made it happen. So, how does that feel?

Envisioning these details is super important for your follow through and, as we said before, your deep motivation level.

Another note about vision boards: feel free to update them whenever you need. Our dreams and goals change as we go along.

LAW OF ATTRACTION FOR MOTIVATION

Sometimes, we are meant to pursue something that in the end is not what we wanted, however, it gets us on the path to what we really want. Remember, you don't fail, you either succeed, or you learn.

To figure out the best career that will bring you joy and abundance, it may take a few different paths to try to see what you like. To find the passionate relationship you have always wanted to be in, it may require dating different people so that you can find out what exactly you are looking for.

Finally, to create a healthy eating plan you enjoy, it may take trying various diets or meal plans from different nutritionists so that eventually you create your own balanced diet plan that you like. The most important thing is not to stop. Keep learning. You are always getting closer and closer to your vision.

Also, show the Universe how committed you are by checking in with your vision board, preferably daily. As we said before, the best thing you can do is to put it in a prominent place where you can see it often.

Follow these steps and behold, your vision will start to play out in numerous ways you never could have imagined. Suddenly you will feel like you have the "third eye" or a higher sense of awareness because you can now see what has always been around, but you could not see before. That is what creating true motivation using the Law of Attraction will do for you.

I cannot wait for you to try this!

What if you still have no idea what to put on your vision board? Or what if you have so many ideas and you feel confused (and you don't want to confuse the Universe too, right) ?

Here are some suggestions:

In your mind, go back to when you were a kid. After all, we all still have a kid inside us *somewhere.* So, what did you like to do when you were younger? What made the time pass quickly over the weekend or the summer vacation from school? What got you excited about your day? Was it drawing, arts, sports, music?

Whatever it was, think about how you could bring more elements of those desired activities into your daily life. Could you sign up for music lessons as an adult? It all counts big time when it comes to making your vision board.

Another idea about how to figure out your dreams and visions is to imagine yourself at the end of your life. This one is a little harder, but definitely worth a try. Yes, at the end of your life, what would you like to have accomplished or seen played out in your lifetime that you would have liked to have been a part of? Use this exercise to influence what you want to put on your vision board.

Additionally, think about what you would have told your current self at the end of your life. For example, I can tend to be a bit of a worrier. *Am I doing it right, am I going to succeed?* I catch myself worrying about these things often.

In my older life, though, I imagine elderly-self telling my current self to *not worry*, but rather enjoy the ride a bit more. So then, I could incorporate elements of what it's like to enjoy life more into my vision and vision board.

This exercise will help you prioritize your vision-to-do list, as well. We only have so much time on this earth, much of it not to be taken for granted. So, what are the more important things – or things that are more important to *you* that you would like to achieve in the next few months, year, five years, etc.? And what can you let fall by the wayside?

I really hope you have an awesome time with your vision board. Give yourself permission to be a kid again for an evening and really imagine a new and improved life for yourself and/or your family. And enjoy!
To help you organize your thoughts and speed up the process of creating your ultimate vision as well as motivational action plan

that aligns with it, you may be interested in using one of our journals, including: *Law of Attraction for Abundance Journal* and *Gratitude Amplifier Journal.*

You will find them at:

www.LOAforSuccess.com/journals

Chapter 3

The # 1 Motivation Killer and How to Mindfully Release It to Live Your Best Life

One of the biggest motivation killers is not the feeling of lack of motivation. It's a feeling of feeling guilty about not feeling motivated or mentally energized all the time.

That feeling also very often appears when you keep comparing yourself to other people and their (very often meticulously fabricated) success stories shown on social media. Don't get me wrong, even if the story is true, the way it is presented might be designed to make you feel inferior and not worthy.

Remember though, it's you and only you who is in control of your life, your actions and your motivation. You are the owner of your blank canvas. And with a blank canvas, you now have the capacity to welcome in the multitude of wonderful, positive, motivational, inspirational attributes of YOU that already exist and are waiting to be expressed.

LAW OF ATTRACTION FOR MOTIVATION

The power of the Law of Attraction is triggered by love (including self-love). And here's the deal with self-love. Self-love is a little addictive – a drug in the best way possible. But what's amazing is that you *can never have* too much of it.

By loving yourself, you allow yourself to be the creator of the story of your life. You can start fresh and create the life that *you* want for yourself. *You.* Not your family, friends or some guru. *You.* Everyone is different and everyone has a different story. Everyone has their own strengths as well as weaknesses.

We are conditioned to celebrate strengths and wins and yea it's a great habit. Give yourself credit for your past accomplishments, no matter how small. But...it's also important to celebrate failure and learn from it. Change the meaning of *failing* to *learning*.

It always takes some time to see a bigger picture. Perhaps you didn't get a job you really wanted to get. You felt disappointed by that circumstance, however, after a few months you discovered a new, more exciting career opportunity and eventually came to the conclusion, "Wow. Thank God I didn't get that job back then. It's the best thing that ever happened to me!"

To stay motivated, you need to own and control your mind. Be like a filter. Think for yourself.

LAW OF ATTRACTION FOR MOTIVATION

Give yourself some time to answer the following questions:

-What are the main things I want to happen in my life?

-What do I want out of life?

- What kind of story do I want to tell about myself, my life?

-What are the circumstances that I used to view as negative but now see as the best thing that ever happened to me?

-What is the feeling I get when I think about those circumstances? A relief? Joy? Abundance? Motivation?

-Was it really worth so much worry?

Now, take some time to have a look at what you consider negative circumstances that are happening to you now. The goal of this exercise is to imagine you are the New, More Empowered Version of You from the future and you are giving the Current You some tips and advice to stay patient.

To take it one step further, fill in the following sentence:

Right now, I am a bit worried about……

LAW OF ATTRACTION FOR MOTIVATION

Yes, allow yourself to express what is worrying you.

Now, finish the following sentence:

But I know there is a reason for my worry because...

I know that all my effort, pain and suffering will eventually get some meaning....

Allow yourself to finish your own story. See everything as a movie where you are in full control of the characters and plot.

Assessing the above questions forces you to do some serious thinking about what is important to you, as well as your motivation.

If you don't know what you want to do in your life and you are still looking for your passion and purpose, don't let that stop you. Make it your motivation to find your purpose and have fun in the process.

The one thing you should avoid is saying, "Other people are motivated because they know what they want. I still don't know my purpose."

LAW OF ATTRACTION FOR MOTIVATION

I have been there so many times, comparing myself to other people. I thought there was some time or even age limit where you were supposed to know your purpose and meaning. Just like I used to think that there was a time limit to where you were supposed to have a certain career and be making certain amount of money, live in a certain house and drive a certain car.

The question is- is it your motivation? If it's from other people, it will not last long.

Whenever you encounter a mental block or are feeling stuck or come up with negative self-talk such as: "I don't know how to do it", "I am not good enough", "I am not as good as…" remember that these are motivation killers. You have the power to get rid of them by using self-love. You can transform the negative self-talk into empowering questions, such as:

"Who can help me/ teach me how to …?"

"What can I do right here, right now to get better at…?"

"What can I do to move forward?"

"How can I attract a great mentor into my life?"

LAW OF ATTRACTION FOR MOTIVATION

Your mind is like a search engine. Be sure to ask good, empowering questions. This step works very well when applied after the first two steps in the book (designing your ideal day and creating your ultimate vision board).

Right now, you are working with long-term intrinsic motivation, which is the most authentic kind of motivation you can align yourself to.

Intrinsic vs Extrinsic Motivation

So, what is the difference between intrinsic and extrinsic motivation? And why is intrinsic motivation preferred for long-term success?

Let's have a look:

Intrinsic motivation- deep, lasting motivation connected to your authentic vision and your core. It is the mother of all motivation and should be paid special attention to.

Intrinsic motivation focuses on:
-What you believe in
-What you love /hate
-What makes you connect with other people

Intrinsic motivation is the root of sustained desire, which, as we all know, is incredibly important to pay attention to when getting stuff done.

Now, let's have a look at *extrinsic motivation.*

You know, it's when you want something so that you can show your achievements on social media. It may keep you going for a

LAW OF ATTRACTION FOR MOTIVATION

while, until you burn out, or you achieve your goals but will feel depleted of fulfillment.

Extrinsic motivation focuses on satisfaction happening more on the exterior, or surface level:
-Appearances
- Money
-Praise from others

Extrinsic motivation surely works but it can help you stay motivated only for a short period of time.

Multiple studies have shown that it is intrinsic motivation, sustained desire, that really gets you to your goals.

Example: Going to the gym

If you are *intrinsically motivated*, you work out because it feels good to go to the gym, it elevates your mood, and you feel healthy. You know you are investing in your wellbeing for years to come.

If you work with *extrinsic motivations* you want to look hot and shredded, or toned, preferably as fast as possible.

LAW OF ATTRACTION FOR MOTIVATION

Don't get me wrong, both scenarios can be motivating, but, from my personal experience, the difference is that intrinsic motivation sets you up for long-term success.

Back to the above-mentioned gym example:

If your only motivation is looking hot, you may be tempted to stop going to the gym as soon as you hit your goal. Some people may even feel tempted to experiment with weight loss pills and some supplements (legal or illegal) that are not always healthy, just to keep their shredded look.

However, if you focus on your core and your intrinsic motivation of going to the gym such as:

-feeling good
-getting rid of stress in a healthy way
-setting up a good, healthy example to other people
-using fitness to build up your discipline and mindset
-staying fit to focus on vitality and longevity and optimize your health

You will not be that likely to quit because fitness will be a part of you, it will be your lifestyle.

Another example: starting a business.

LAW OF ATTRACTION FOR MOTIVATION

If a person is only driven by extrinsic motivation and some kind of an entrepreneur status to show on social media, they may burn out after reaching a certain financial milestone. Some individuals who are driven entirely by money and want to make it as fast as possible, may even turn to illegal or unethical activities, just to make their money quickly and they may lose their business.

However, if a person has a deep *why* behind their actions and can access their internal motivations such as:
-create products and services that really help people
-set a good example to other entrepreneurs
-grow their business to be able to offer jobs in their local community
-be a true expert in their field and grow their knowledge while helping other people

Then, they will keep going and going uphill even if they encounter some obstacles on their journey.

All world-famous bestselling authors have written dozens if not hundreds of manuscripts before their career took off. They kept going because they were truly passionate about writing and creating their characters while providing entertainment and escapism for their readers. That was their goal and motivation. Had their only motivation been to become an instant bestseller, they would have quit after a few rejected manuscripts.

LAW OF ATTRACTION FOR MOTIVATION

So now that you have a blank canvas and are aware of some of your intrinsic and extrinsic motivations, let's take those and apply them to our metaphor of painting a life picture filled with deliberate self-love and care.

You now know what motivates you, both on the inside and out. Let's take those motivations, knead them a bit, and lay them out for the base of your story – one immersed in self-love and desire...

Remember it's okay to use a bit of extrinsic motivation and a bit of ego here and there. Just do not allow it to be your only source of motivation. Yes, it will feel nice to lose weight, get toned, and reward yourself by buying some new clothes and posting a selfie on social media. If that helps you get started- do it. If it helps you keep going by documenting your journey and you enjoy sharing what you do with other people and you feel it gives you extra motivation- do it. Why not?

Remember though- the best motivation is your intrinsic one.

The following questions and exercises will help you access your intrinsic motivations for all areas of your life.

Be sure to give yourself some time and space to go through the following set of questions several times. Each time do it in the context of a different area of your life such as

-Health & Fitness

-Career & Work

-Family & Friends

-Love & Relationships

-Money & Finance etc.

Questions:

-How do I see myself in the next five years?

-What does the New, More Empowered Version of me do?

-What do I want to change in the world?

-What makes me happy?

-What annoys me?

-What do I want to be remembered for?

-How do I want to inspire other people?

-What do I want to be known for?

The Self-Love for Motivation

I am sure you are probably wondering, "What is the connection between the Law of Attraction, motivation and self-love?"

Well, here's a traditional self-development "formula":

LAW OF ATTRACTION FOR MOTIVATION

Motivation -> action - > results - > self-worth and self-love stemming from achievement

You somehow get motivated, you take action, and get results. Then you start feeling good about yourself.

It looks logical and innocent, but...nobody talks about possible consequences.

Action -> results - > lack of results - >failure -> shame -> feeling worthless -> losing motivation

It basically means that if you take action from a place of lack, even though you may create some results, they will not last long. They will turn to what you perceive as failure which leads to shame, guilt and eventually a loss of motivation.

Here's my preferred formula, please note it leaves lots of space for different variations. I always say there is no fixed blueprint. I like flexible blueprints that can be adjusted depending on a person's needs and preferences:

Self-love -> energy of abundance and fulfillment –> full alignment –> fusing yourself with your goals –> meaningful action aligned with intrinsic motivation- >repeat and enjoy!

LAW OF ATTRACTION FOR MOTIVATION

The only thing you can actually afford to chase is self-love. You don't need other people's permission or approval and you have the right to be yourself.

I am now going to get to the "nitty gritty" on what needs to happen for you to love yourself fully and what tools you can use to access joy, inner-peace, and lasting dedication to your dreams.

Why? Several reasons, most importantly *why not*? Also, self-love – the practice of caring for and about yourself – is the basis not only of your doing well, but once you've satisfied your own needs in terms of care, you will be in a much more giving place to care about others.

We come from a mindset that selflessness is best. "Think of others before you think of yourself", we say. Yes…but also no – at least not in my humble opinion.

Yes, I think about you, my reader. Because of that I want to write good books, hire good editors and narrators. I make sure the team helps me spread my message and that they are also passionate about it. But to do that, I need to put myself first. I need to take care of my body and mind. I need to eat healthily, be in bed early and wake up early so that I can write when my productivity is at its peak, and before I have to work on other projects.

When I commit to writing, I make sure I stay hydrated, get enough sleep and switch off all my devices and email. I answer emails from my readers only after I am done writing. Otherwise, I would not be able to help anyone.

Of course, there are some circumstances in which we need to think of others before ourselves, but the vast majority of giving, thorough, honest and genuine giving comes from a place of feeling satisfied and full ourselves.

Here are a few tips on how to use self-love to stay motivated:

-Forgive Yourself (Stop Dwelling on Failures)

We already discussed this in brief, but let's take it a little further. You can change the thoughts and words in your head into empowering questions that will stimulate your subconscious mind.

Negative self-talk and self-guilt such as, "Why do I always fail?", "I will never be successful at this", become
"Who can help me with this?" and "What can I do to learn how to do this?"

Eventually, you will start turning those small empowering questions into small consistent actions, such as:

LAW OF ATTRACTION FOR MOTIVATION

-using two hours every evening to work on a new business, or learning a new skill. Perhaps you will start waking up one hour earlier to write that book you have always wanted to write or work out to feel more energized throughout the day. As you get on what feels like the right track for you, start affirming what you do by using affirmations such as:

-I love waking up early. I am a morning person
-I love working on my new business venture and I am really passionate about it

Practice those small actions to stay in motion. Motion leads to motivation, remember what I said about being patient and impatient at the same time? Be patient about the long-term results, they do take time. But...be impatient and start taking those small, aligned actions to manifest what you want.

What you want to avoid are mindless affirmations, taken from a place of lack and scarcity. You want to feel totally fused with your goals, not separated from them. Separation will eventually result in a lack of motivation and we don't want that to happen.

These shifts are really, really cool to experience, especially as they start to happen.

LAW OF ATTRACTION FOR MOTIVATION

In order to move past mental blocks, you need to thoroughly and unconditionally forgive yourself. One of the reasons you can't get started may be that you are scared. Something went wrong in the past and your natural reaction is fear. It took me a while to work through it and really believe it. Now I feel it. I totally accept the fact that every project is a process that involves making mistakes. Perfection does not exist but there is an art of balancing.

Guilt is an absolutely wasted emotion. Sitting around and feeling guilty does nothing but add toxic elements to your existence (not to mention your energy) and is beyond detrimental to your recovery and life improvement journey. Yes, allow yourself to feel guilty. Just make sure that you set a timer and ask yourself- how long do I want to feel down for? Feel bad for a few minutes, but then ditch that guilt. Have a short-term memory about whatever it is you're feeling guilty about.

Take Some You-Time

I remember teaching this process to an entrepreneur friend of mine. The guy was a big fan of a non-stop hustle and he kept going until he burned out.

It was a very hard task to teach him the process of self-care and self-love. He just had this idea he neeed to be productive. Once he released that guilt though, he saw his business ventures in a new light and changed his relationship with motivation.

Once you have released your guilt, it is time to take the time for YOU that you need. This may sound unrealistic, depending on your circumstances, but taking the time to dream and let what you love about life soak in, is absolutely necessary for welcoming improvements into your life.

Now, I realize that most of us are busy. Time is scarce. We have obligations, families, events, social lives, work commitments, etc. Who has the time to sit around and dream, you may ask! Well... you do! It just takes a tiny bit of astuteness, intuition and a little efficiently appropriated time.

YOU time is a huge part of writing your self-love-filled life story. (And again, even if you can't take that time in large quantities, make what you can do count. And count big.) If we don't take the time for ourselves, we will run on empty, sputter, and eventually run out of gas. This empty frenetic energy is what makes people so unmotivated.

LAW OF ATTRACTION FOR MOTIVATION

The Art of Saying *No*

This one can get pretty hard. Especially if your goal is to be a kind, loving person who never says *no*. But here's the gist: do not overcommit. Say *no* to things that do not align with your vision. You can still do it from a place of kindness. If you want to be in charge of your life, you need to set boundaries. As you keep pursuing your goals, people who are your true friends will be inspired by what you do and will want to do the same.

Saying *no* to things that aren't your responsibility is actually quite empowering! Most people will feel inspired by the fact that you have goals and an agenda to follow and that you are working on something big.

Trust the Process and Love Every Minute of it.

Ah, patience. Be patient, my friend. Challenges are just hidden opportunities. Your awareness in this present moment is much higher than it was, for example, five years ago. When you look back at something that happened to you several years ago, something you used to look at as a failure, your current state of awareness may see it as a blessing.

LAW OF ATTRACTION FOR MOTIVATION

Use this mechanism to ease temporary pain or disappointments that, let's face it, are inevitable. In five or ten years' time, your sense of awareness and perception will be higher than it is now, and what you now see as struggle will seem like a blessing to you.

Chapter 4

The Mental and Emotional Peeling to Welcome the New and Get Rid of the Old

Improving your relationship with yourself is proportional to improving your motivation. Most people don't really struggle with motivation, they struggle with their self-image.

Success is not about achieving what other people expect you to do and it's not about fitting in. Success is about having the courage to be yourself.

Learning (or re-learning) how to love yourself.

The Law of Attraction magnifies what you constantly focus on. So, constant negative self-talk and torturing yourself with:

-I am not motivated

-I am not good enough

-I don't know how

LAW OF ATTRACTION FOR MOTIVATION

will only amplify the negativity in your life while destroying your motivation.

We must first, as the saying goes, go "out with the old". In other words, let's figure out – and then ditch – our pervasive and unhelpful self-talk habits. Think of it as an emotional and mental peeling. You have the power to get rid of the layers that are holding you back from living your true potential.

It's time to turn negative into positive and align your energy, actions and thoughts with your vision.

The first step here is to notice how you talk to yourself. Notice -- *What am I saying to myself?* Simply notice.

Note: Do not make judgments or analyze this self-talk – yet. For some reason, we love to beat ourselves up about minor and/or insignificant details such as saying something stupid in a meeting, or not saying what we really wanted to say.

Throughout the next day or two, make a small list with two or three negative things you say to yourself daily. Read it often – and, again, *without judgment*. Simply say:

"I say _____ to myself often" – and leave it at that.

LAW OF ATTRACTION FOR MOTIVATION

Transform it into something positive.

The absolute best way to combat negativity in your mind – to get rid of it using our mental and emotional peeling technique– is to reverse the aforementioned negative self-talk with positive affirmations coming from a place of wholeness and abundance.

Now, what you want to do here is take your little list of negative self-talk and next to each negative statement, write a positive affirmation. (An affirmation is a statement expressed in the positive voice, right?)

Let's do an example. Say you constantly tell yourself some negative lines, such as:

"No one will ever hire me because I'm not as smart as other candidates."

First of all, this is not a true statement. It's just a statement but, if you keep repeating it over and over again, it may become your belief, to be precise-your limiting belief.

Now, let's change it.

- "No one will hire me because I'm not as smart as other candidates" will now become:

LAW OF ATTRACTION FOR MOTIVATION

- "I am smart and bright, and there are thousands of people who would love to hire me very soon."

Let's take it even further:
"Because I am so smart and dedicated, I am passionate about learning. I love taking professional courses and increasing my qualifications."

Now, if you decide to enroll in a professional course, coming from this Passion Mindset ("I love it, I study because I am passionate about learning" etc.), you are bound to be successful and fulfilled and your motivation will be long-term.

However, if you pursue education from a place of feeling unworthy and not being good enough, chances are you will translate the same pattern into a new environment, whether it's a work place, gym, or a professional course you want to take.

But what if it's not true, you might be thinking. *I'm not smart or bright or about to be hired...*

The thing about affirmations is that you write them NO MATTER WHAT YOU THINK. It's a tough pill to swallow, but your perception may be off anyway. Trust that there is a world out there in which thousands of people would love to hire you very soon.

LAW OF ATTRACTION FOR MOTIVATION

Another example: "I can't go to the gym because I'm out of shape and I will look so stupid."

So, let's rewrite this story into something more empowering:
"I love working on my body and aligning myself with the new, healthy version of myself", or "my body loves the gym and so does my mind!"

Again, even if you doubt these affirmations (or this process) with every fiber in your body, continue to write them. Do it anyway. Brainwash yourself (in a good way of course).

When it comes to being the hero of your own life and/or the author of your own story, affirmations are worth spending time on.

There is no right or wrong. The only right way of doing your affirmations is what makes you feel good in a given moment.

Put some passion into these, even if it's hard or you don't want to, and write these awesome, positive statements down as frequently as possible – in a notebook, on a napkin. Just do them and do them *often*.

LAW OF ATTRACTION FOR MOTIVATION

Releasing Pressure and Judgment to Feel Free and Naturally Motivated

Let's face it…we have all been guilty of judging others.
For me personally, I was as strict on myself as I was on other people. I was confusing high standards and true ambition with high pressure. Unnecessarily high pressure.

A former mentor of mine whom I deeply trusted back then had taught me to be like this and since I had no clue about "owning and controlling my mind" I had made the mistake of blindly following through. That led me on a path of self-destruction as well as criticizing others. I would spend at least a few hours a day thinking or saying negative things about myself and other people. Caught up in unnecessary gossip, I was hurting others and myself.

Since I was in a non-stop judgment and criticism mindset, I was constantly afraid that others would judge me too, and needless to say, my negative energy was coming back to me all the time. I felt drained and could not find the motivation to purse my true goals, goals I was passionate about.

Finally, I realized I was wasting my time and energy that could be spent on something more positive and empowering, such as doing inner work, meditating or taking care of my body. I decided to go on a "judgement detox" and it worked really well.

LAW OF ATTRACTION FOR MOTIVATION

At first, I vowed to myself that I would stop judging myself about feeling judgmental. Instead, I decided to simply become aware of my feelings and thoughts. I decided to catch onto the negative patterns.

Whenever I felt like criticizing someone, or I had a gossip friend of mine criticize someone else, I made a conscious effort to turn it into a positive statement by finding something good to say about a person, situation and myself. It all began by rearranging my wording and creating a new, empowering habit. That one simple step led me to increased energy and motivation.

At the time of my transformation, I was running a small business where I was managing a team of several employees. When I changed from a strict and judgmental high-pressure mindset to an understanding and positive mindset I was able to communicate much better with the team I was managing and increase their motivation too. Whenever I had to give someone feedback, I made a conscious decision to first remind them about their true potential and what they did well instead of being judgmental about what they do. I could give them honest feedback in a way that was motivating and empowering.

That change however, started with myself and how I talked with myself. To motivate others, you must first understand your own motivation. What is happening to you and around you is a reflection of your inner world. And you can shift your inner world to any place you like.

Remember…it all starts with self-love and using it to erase self-judgment. You take action because it feels good and because you enjoy it. You don't need to use pressure (on yourself or others) to achieve your goals and to be happy.

A positive self-image is the gateway to some awesome self-love coming your way. It also helps you attract people who are on the same vibration. So, pay attention to where you can throw in some positive self-talk to describe your efforts. It may seem weird at first, and like it's not helping you. But over time, you will learn that less value judgment in the short term equals incredible self-motivation in the longer term.

You are enough, and your efforts are fabulous. You are also a beacon of light, so keep going forward and acting as such. Adjusting your wording will help you write or re-write this aspect of your newly changed, more self-actualized story. Deciding to ditch the value judgments gives you longevity in your thinking, flexibility in your perception, and creativity to expand the lenses through which you see the world.

Chapter 5

How to Deal with Adversity and Keep Taking Inspired Action

To create a positive, lasting change and unleash your deep motivation, you must also accept the negative. Have no fear though- we will have a look at the negative in a very empowering way to make you stronger and to make sure your motivation muscle is so powerful that nobody and nothing can stop you.

One truth to accept is that as you change and grow and become even more transformed in this process, you might come up against a few challenging situations.

How to Deal with People who Question Your Journey

When we decide to transform, if others, specifically friends and family, remain where they are, they may not exactly understand the changes we are working on to create our best lives. In some cases, they may even try to slow us down or stop us from moving forward. Unfortunately, sometimes people get so used to our being the way we have always been, even if that way is a bit "blocked". As we liberate our own minds and spirits, it seems a bit scary for other people. As we evolve and create exciting visions while taking action to align with what we want, it feels like we no longer fit into the mold that our closest ones are so used to seeing us in.

In most cases, our family and friends still love and care for us, so we need to be patient with their reactions. It's not that they want to criticize us, it's just they may fear we are "getting too big" or "acting weird". Maybe they don't want us to get hurt. Again, just understand where they are coming from. Be grateful that other people care about you but remember that your motivations are different than theirs. It's okay to be different and to work on something that other people may not understand.

Also remember that as you keep going and getting closer to your vision by taking meaningful action and manifesting the reality you want, those who truly care about you and wish you well will be inspired by your transformation.

In fact, one of my motivations I still use to do my daily writing sessions and my daily workouts is:

"I do it to inspire and motivate those around me."

But it wasn't always like that. When I first got started on my transformational journey, most of my friends and family thought I had lost it. Some would even make jokes about me and my work.

LAW OF ATTRACTION FOR MOTIVATION

However, I decided to be patient, listen to my inner voice and just ignore certain remarks. By reacting to them, I knew I would attract more of that negative energy and it would have a negative impact on my motivation. What you focus on, you attract more of.

Had I listened to what other people were telling me, I would have never transformed my health and I would have never gotten into writing. After years of feeling disconnected from myself, I began asking myself what was happening and why I could never follow through on my real dreams and ambitions.

By using the process, I described in the earlier chapters, I quickly realized that I had way too many negative voices in my head and these were becoming my excuses. I quickly identified all those negative voices as well as the limiting beliefs that were pretty much coming from other people, including my friends and family, and were installed on my hard drive after so many years of feeling disconnected from my vision and goals.

But here's the thing: you cannot just remove a limiting belief and hope for the best. You need to replace the limiting belief with an empowering belief.

For example, the beliefs I got from my family:
- "If you work out you won't have time for your family."
- "Eating healthily is only for rich people."

- "Eating healthily doesn't taste good anyway, come on, you gotta have something good in your life. Life is already hard enough."

I began replacing these with self-love and empowerment, one by one. For example, instead of, "If you are always working out, you won't have time for the family", I said, "You can both work out and hang out with family and friends."

I began organizing hiking trips that were fun. I would get some of my friends and family members and we would just walk in nature, burn calories and have fun. We could still catch up, but instead of going to a bar, we would get some fresh air, admire nature or even join a yoga workshop. Then, eventually, we felt inspired to combine our hikes with eating healthy food.

Aside from that, I realized that health is the most valuable asset we have. I can still remember what it felt like when I could not get up and felt absolutely powerless. The doctors just prescribed antidepressants, but the truth is that my body lacked a healthy, clean diet and exercise.

Now, I have never been a gym person. So, I decided to focus on other activities, mostly in nature, like hiking, for example. I also joined yoga and Pilates classes. I gradually added more positive changes. I kept track of my progress. I still allowed myself to get off track every now and then. That is absolutely fine. You don't want to be too strict on yourself. It's better to focus on your long-term vision.

Eventually, I really started enjoying my hikes. Getting outdoors in the fresh air felt amazing. I loved my hikes so much that I decided to take them to another level, and I began jogging. Another change and shift added gradually. Had I vowed to jog every day at the beginning of my journey, I wouldn't have had any success with it. I would have worked on willpower alone. And that can only last so long.

A friend of mine, who was going through the same process, decided to transform his health and fitness as well. Aside from that, he became very inspired by what I was doing with my writing. His challenge was time, because he had a full-time job and a family to support. But he managed to do it anyway. He started small. He started waking up ten to fifteen minutes earlier and doing some simple exercises that required no equipment. Just watching YouTube videos and following online fitness courses and DVDs. He made a small commitment that only took fifteen minutes a day, every day, first thing in the morning, before things became too hectic.

His old limiting belief had been that if you had a full-time job and a family to support, and you wanted to be a good dad, you had to give up on your passions because continuing with them would be egoistical. He had heard this from his dad, his uncle, and his grandpa. But his new, empowering belief, fueled by self-love, was this:

"As a good dad, I need to take care of my health and fitness and set a good example to my family. This also allows me to be more productive at work and increases my chances of getting a promotion."

So, he kept going. Eventually, he started waking up even earlier and added more exercises to do in the morning because it felt so good. His wife also became inspired to do fitness training.
Then he decided to add another habit. While at work, he had a one-hour lunch break. He didn't need a full hour to eat anyway. He could enjoy his lunch within twenty minutes, and then instead of browsing through his phone, he decided to focus on writing. He soon realized that half an hour a day can be easily turned into a thousand words. That's thirty thousand words a month which can be a short novella or a smaller size nonfiction book.

Think beyond yourself, your mission, your purpose. Beyond the work you are meant to be doing. Who did you allow to enter your mind and why? Perhaps you fear it will be hard or that it will take too long, or that you will get laughed at. You can help other people by becoming the best version of yourself starting right here and now. You don't need to wait for the perfect moment. Be yourself and shine your light. Also, give yourself permission to move at your own pace. Remember, you don't fail - you succeed, or you learn.

Careful with Toxic People Though

As you make changes and self-improvements on your journey, watch out for the person in your life who suddenly becomes very needy for your time and attention. Perhaps they were always needy, and you didn't realize it, or perhaps they are subconsciously noticing your changes and becoming a little scared.

Either way, assess to what degree these people still fit into your life. You may need to distance yourself from them for a while, and that is fine. You need to protect your mind, energy and vision. Do what you need to do for *you*.

It's up to you to be in charge of whether you can afford to have any "toxic" personalities in your life. Decide in what capacity you can handle them *without* them interfering with your journey and progress.

How to Deal with Self-Sabotage

Another thing you need to be mentally and emotionally prepared for is self-sabotage.

When you are motivated to make some amazing changes in your life, and your vision and purpose are being actualized, your old self may decide to make a comeback to get you back to the old reality. It can happen if you are not careful.

It's called self-sabotage.

Self-sabotage comes from your mind's scared place that subconsciously tells you that staying motivated to manifest your own greatness is not something you should pursue, so you try to stop yourself, whether on purpose or not.

Here's a simple example from my life. For a very long time, whenever things would start to go well in my life, I would get very sick. A cold, the flu, some random allergy or food poisoning. But no matter how I tried to change it, every time I manifested something great, I had to "get back to earth" and it felt like a vicious cycle of waking up from a wonderful dream. That thing became a pattern.

I would end up on these doctors' visits, one after the other, thinking something was really wrong, and they would tell me it was a virus, or some digestive issue, or that I just needed some rest and more sleep. And they were right. My self-imposed sabotage would always lead me to staying up late, going out and drinking where I should have rested. These negative patterns were eventually leading me to sickness. I was creating my own sickness, by taking self-sabotaging actions that were out of alignment with my new self and wanted to bring the old me back. The old me that would play it safe.

The point here is that I'd learned this pattern of sabotage early in my life – for whatever reason – and that it was preventing me to create long-lasting changes in my life.

I had to let go. So, I focused on journaling and affirmations to gently center my awareness on the root of the problem by aligning myself with a better self-care. I began paying more attention to my impulsive actions like having that one more glass of wine when I should have had a soft drink instead, or ordering some junk food when I should have gone for a salad. It may seem like not a big deal but all those small, self-sabotaging actions combined, would make me get sick on a regular basis, especially when I was close to manifesting a big success. It's like this old self desperately trying to put the new self back behind the curtain.

LAW OF ATTRACTION FOR MOTIVATION

Back then, I knew I had to regain my power and re-work my negative and self-sabotaging actions so I changed my affirmations to include statements about a healthy body and mind and how I loved myself. It took work, lots of work but I no longer would get down the road of manifesting abundance and have to back up after a few weeks just to take care of some annoying ailment.

Don't be afraid to be on the lookout for self-sabotage. You're your own self-awareness detective. Don't judge what is happening. Simply become aware so that you can start taking small actions to turn negative into positive.

Especially as you get closer and closer to achieving some of the items on your vision board, keep a keen eye on your own efforts to subconsciously slow down your progress. Whatever you do, don't give into it. Additionally, we have other people's sabotage efforts to deal with. Remember those toxic friends? Yes, make sure they are not sabotaging you, either. They may even do it without realizing it.

Your Awareness is Your Power

Be mindfully aware of when you get closer to your dream reality. Or even when you get close to a milestone on your journey toward them. A friend might need help with moving to a new house, or a family member may need you for something else, when it's your last opportunity of the day to work on yourself and your vision.

I'm not saying get rid of all responsibility here; but I am saying be aware that this will happen and be very mindful about where you want to spend your time, energy, and efforts. Keep your eyes on your vision – because you absolutely deserve to. One thing I am a huge fan of are mindful morning rituals, and it's something we will be discussing in the next chapter. The best thing you can do for yourself is to do all your important Law of Attraction-Motivational work early in the morning, so that when life gets hectic, you feel grounded and aligned. It feels good to know you start your day by taking care of your vision and it will also allow you to help others to the best of your ability.

Chapter 7

The Best LOA Tools to Stay Motivated

Mindful morning rituals are incredibly important for aligning yourself with your vision and staying motivated throughout the day. Remember- motivation is a muscle and it deserves to be worked on.

If you don't have a Mindful Morning Ritual yet, now is the time to change that. Sleeping past your alarm, skipping your morning smoothie, meditation or self-care will prevent you from creating sustainable energy to help you keep going.

Imagine, that you have an 8:00 a.m. work meeting. You set your alarm for 5:30 a.m. with intent on hitting the gym, cooking a light breakfast, taking a shower and driving to work. But unfortunately, you hit snooze, hit snooze again, then again. Before you know it, it's 7:00 a.m. and you've missed your time to work out, so you jump out of bed, hit the shower, skip breakfast and rush to get to work.

You are a little groggy still, flustered, and feeling guilty about not working out. You haven't taken the proper time for yourself to set up an amazing day. And your energy around your workplace reflects it.

LAW OF ATTRACTION FOR MOTIVATION

Eventually, that negative energy actually attracts more negativity into your day, and you begin wondering why you are losing your motivation.

Setting yourself up for success first thing in the morning is the goal here. Running on "doing just what you need to" is low frequency and stepping away from your vision.

Now, before you go to bed, imagine a morning where you wake up on the first buzz of your alarm. You tell yourself that today is going to be an amazing day and that little miracles will take place. You make your bed, brush your teeth, mediate and work out, shower, make a healthy smoothie for breakfast and allow yourself plenty of time to start your day the right way.

The Universe works in mysterious and energy-related ways. So, you might as well set yourself up for the latter.

Mindful Exercises to Raise Your Vibration First Thing in the Morning

Experiment with these exercises. See how they affect you. Don't force yourself to do activities you don't like. Stick to your preferred form of morning ritual.

The Power of Mindful Journaling

Journaling is a tool that can help you get rid of negative emotions such as anger, resentment, and guilt. At the same time, it can help you celebrate your small successes and bring your dreams even closer into your reality. Have a blank journal to write in, right beside your bed. When you wake up, grab it and start writing whatever feels good.

It can be what you are grateful for (give priority to one specific area of life that needs most of your attention, while also being grateful for things, people and circumstances related to other areas of your life as that will bring balance).

For example, if your number one thing you are trying to transform is your career and finances and you want to manifest more abundance, while staying motivated to pursue your deep ambitions, start off by writing what you are already grateful for when it comes to your professional life. What are your achievements? You can also be grateful for something you haven't achieved yet, in fact, it's very powerful.

Then, be sure to quickly scan other areas of your life and be grateful for your health, relationships and family. Balance is very important, and you don't want to get too caught up in only one area of your life.

Some days you may be too busy to write in your journal. And so, what you can do instead, as you drink your morning coffee, is quickly read through what you have written so far. In fact, it's a very powerful, vibration-raising activity that will help you stay aligned with your vision while increasing your *why* and your motivation.

What else can you write about? ANYTHING. EVERYTHING. You can write down your goals in a present tense and feel grateful for them. You can write down a simple action plan for today, to make sure you stay mindfully focused on those small, consistent actions.

At the same time, what journaling allows us to do is to empty our brains of toxic, negative thoughts. We can organize our thoughts and come up with new ideas.

LAW OF ATTRACTION FOR MOTIVATION

Many of my book ideas come from something I wrote in my journal years ago. When I look back, I see certain patterns and thoughts I can turn into processes I get to teach through my books.

Mindful journaling unleashes that feeling of being proactive and filled with joy and positive energy. That is pure motivation, not only for you but also for those around you. Trust me on that one. The good energy you are spreading will come back to you.

LAW OF ATTRACTION FOR MOTIVATION

How to Use Affirmations to Stay Motivated

Have a look at your vision board. What are the things you want to have more of in your life?

Include them in your affirmations and combine them with a feeling of gratitude. For example, if you want more abundance in your life, an affirmation such as, "I am well-compensated for my efforts at work, I attract abundance in all areas of my life, I attract amazing opportunities to my business and life" is something you want to focus on. Be sure to use your affirmations in a mindful way. Feel them, don't just recite them. Also, create them in a way that feels right and powerful for you in a given moment.

At first, it may seem to you that the affirmations don't work or don't do anything. You need to trust the process and be patient. You will realize the power of your efforts when you catch your inner voice guiding you in the right direction.

For example, you feel like skipping your workout or a heathy meal. Then, all of a sudden, the affirmation you've been repeating for so many months comes in to save you, in a very subconscious manner. It tells you:
"Come on! That is not who you are, you love working out, you love fitness, you love going to the gym, you deserve a healthy fit body."

LAW OF ATTRACTION FOR MOTIVATION

This happens only because several months earlier, you mindfully created an affirmation that said, "I deserve a healthy, fit body and I just love going to the gym."

Or perhaps you are on a call with a client. Your old self feels like undercharging for your services. But, then, you receive the guidance from the new, more empowered version of you that tells you:

"Wait, that's not who you are! You deserve to charge more. People will appreciate your services and will want more of them."

This happens because you mindfully came up with a powerful affirmation that said, "I attract amazing clients who value my work and are happy to pay higher prices. I deserve a business I love, and I deserve abundance through the work I do."

Again, choose an affirmation that speaks to you in a positive way, or even an affirmation to which you have a negative or uncomfortable reaction. It's okay, because sometimes a strong negative reaction towards an affirmation or area of weakness means we need to really work on that specific area. The best emotional and long-lasting motivational growth happens here.

Write the affirmation over and over again. You can also record it and listen to it while you are doing some things around the house.

LAW OF ATTRACTION FOR MOTIVATION

At first, it will feel weird, even a bit uncomfortable to listen to yourself (unless, of course, your profession is around acting, singing or being a voice artist). But, any feeling of discomfort is temporary and will soon offer you unexpected empowerment exactly when you need it.

Meditation to Stay Motivated?

This one is my favorite and you can easily do it, even if you are new to meditation. All you need to get started is the willingness to give your mind some space to let go of distractions.

Think: five minutes of quiet time, when you can be free and just focus on you.

Before you begin your meditation, start with an intention. For example:

"I am relaxed."
"I am focused."
"I am productive."
"I enjoy my dream house."

LAW OF ATTRACTION FOR MOTIVATION

You can also focus on your ultimate vision, and in your mind, go through various pictures from your vision board. Then, with your intention in mind, simply sit somewhere in your room or outside in nature, it's totally up to you.

Sit cross-legged or in a way that feels good. Breathe slowly and deliberately, but don't force anything, just let it come. Focus on your breath. Breathe in and out, in and out. Picture the air going into your lungs, resting there for a second and then moving out.

When any stressful thoughts creep in, relax, accept them and go back to focusing on your breath. Meditation is a fantastic and very often under-valued tool to work on your motivation muscle. You see, meditation is about gently overcoming distractions by accepting them and bringing the focus back to your main thing, which, in the case of meditation is your breath.

Just like in life, there will be distractions, toxic people and circumstances to put you to test, but you will be prepared to accept them. You won't feel guilty about them and you will just go back to doing your main thing- getting closer to manifesting your vision.

So, meditate and don't worry if your mind wanders, it's normal. Keep breathing in and out. Like a steady heartbeat. Take at least five minutes a day to mediate and always be sure to start off with one clean intention.

LAW OF ATTRACTION FOR MOTIVATION

I know what you're thinking…Meditation for motivation? Really?

After all, doesn't meditation have to do with just resting and being content? And if motivation is anything, it's the drive to achieve or gain something, right?

But meditation is about more than contentment and peace of mind. Meditation is about clarity and living in an honest, straightforward relation to your world. Meditation does not just make a permanent dent on your cushion. It also makes a deep impact on the way you live your life and how you get and stay motivated. Besides, things go better when you are at peace with yourself.

I know it can be challenging to find some self-care time for yourself. But something is better than nothing. Two minutes a day, every day will eventually compound. Just like with any goal in life- it doesn't have to be all or nothing. Focus on the baby steps and enjoy the process.

Even if you meditate a few minutes before you go to bed, that works too and you can set an intention to rest well, reconnect with your vision and even allow your subconscious mind to give you answers to your questions while you sleep. By allowing yourself to close your eyes and meditate before you go to sleep, not only will you sleep better but you will also wake up more energized and happier the next day.

Also, give yourself some space to experiment to see what works for you: Each and every one of these rituals is, well…. a *ritual*. You can't run a marathon without training, just like you can't change your life or do a 180 on one aspect of your life overnight. It's one small baby step at a time. Over time, the transformation will come.

Throughout my ongoing journey of holistic self-help and spirituality, the lesson of ditching perfection for progress has been the hardest one to learn. When I first got started on mindful morning rituals, I would do one day of the practices from this chapter, not see a ton of change right away and give up, feeling like a loser. Nope, nope. Doesn't work that way.

The trick is always, "slow and steady wins the race". Start off with just a mini five minute mindful morning ritual you can commit to.

See how you feel. For example, you can start off with journaling, then add in the affirmations, then the meditation. Or start off with whatever practice you feel attracted to now. Listen to your body and mind, they have all the answers. Follow your instincts. You can even keep switching between your favorite practices, so that you don't get bored. The essence of doing all this is basically to grow your motivation muscle by aligning yourself with your core and your ultimate vision on a daily basis. It's about following up with a simple, daily action plan that feels good and natural for you.

Pretty soon, you'll have an awesome morning routine that will keep you in the moment, present, and ready to take on life's challenges at their core. At your core. Because your core is strong and ready for the tasks at hand.

Conclusion

Be yourself. Embrace your uniqueness. Be the best you that you can be. Do *not*, for any reason, settle for less.

We can elevate our frequency and push ourselves to be even better simply by working on our beliefs and inner game.

When things don't go your way, allow yourself to take a step back. Revise your vision, drive and motivation. Go through the exercises from this book several times. Are you still going in the direction you truly desire? Continue to stay the course, even though occasionally it may need to be revised.

Reality will win out if you let it, so think big. Think vast. Think tall and wide and deep and thoroughly. Know that you have the power to change someone's life and, most specifically, your own. Understand the value in that. And then go out and spread the love. Love conquers fear. Love unleashes your power and unstoppable motivation.

We get one life. One. Get serious about changing it for the better. Because you truly can, you deserve to, and the world is a much better place because of your transformation that inspires those around you.

LAW OF ATTRACTION FOR MOTIVATION

Motivation and happiness can be found through many avenues and for all of them the journey itself is usually the joy. The destination is what we want to achieve, but it is in getting there that we constantly find out more about ourselves and our own uniqueness.

It's the process that makes us stronger and grows our motivation muscle while helping us transform on a deeper level. And this is the most fascinating of all. Who you become in the process of learning about your vision, ambitions, and motivations.

Until we meet again in another book – be motivated, be happy, be strong inside and out.

Sending you lots of love from here.
Love, Elena

Questions?
You can reach out to me via my blog:

www.LOAforSuccess.com

info@loaforsuccess.com

Elena G.Rivers

LAW OF ATTRACTION FOR MOTIVATION

A Special Offer from Elena

Finally, I would like to invite you to join my private mailing list (my **VIP LOA Newsletter**). Whenever I release a new book, you will be able to get it at a discounted price (or sometimes even for free, but don't tell anyone 😉).

In the meantime, I will keep you entertained with a free copy of my exclusive LOA workbook that will be emailed to you when you sign up.

LAW OF ATTRACTION FOR MOTIVATION

To join visit the link below now:

www.loaforsuccess.com/home

After you have signed up, you will get a free instant access to this exclusive workbook (+ many other helpful resources that I will be sending you on a regular basis). I hope you will enjoy your free workbook.

If you have any questions, please email us at: support@loaforsuccess.com

LAW OF ATTRACTION FOR MOTIVATION

More Books written by Elena G.Rivers

Available at: www.loaforsuccess.com

Ebook – Paperback – Audiobook Editions Available Now

Law of Attraction for Amazing Relationships

LAW OF ATTRACTION FOR MOTIVATION

Law of Attraction -Manifestation Exercises

Law of Attraction for Abundance

LAW OF ATTRACTION FOR MOTIVATION

Law of Attraction to Make More Money

You will find more at:

www.loaforsuccess.com/books

www.ingramcontent.com/pod-product-compliance
Lightning Source LLC
Chambersburg PA
CBHW071008080526
44587CB00015B/2384